Phalaenopsis Bob gordon

Irma gronborg

BEGINNERS GUIDE TO GROWING

PHALAENOPSIS ORCHIDS

by Bob Gordon

ILLUSTRATIONS BY IRINA GRONBORG

Laid-Back Publications
Rialto, CA 92376
1986

Published by
Laid-Back Publications
Rialto, California, USA

ISBN 0-9615714-2-X

Re-order information, back inside cover

Cover:
Phalaenopsis Kathy Ahrenn "The Graduate"

Printed in the United States of America

Typography by
Archetype Typesetting, Riverside CA

TABLE OF CONTENTS

Dedicated to all who would like to grow orchids,
but never thought they could.

Now they can.

THE PURPOSE OF THIS BOOK:

THIS BOOK IS INTENDED TO GIVE THE READER THE INSTRUCTION AND ENCOURAGEMENT NECESSARY TO GROW AND FLOWER PHALAENOPSIS ORCHID PLANTS SUCCESSFULLY.

It is a basic culture manual that should allay the fears, satisfy most needs, and answer most questions that will arise during the first year of growing the world's most beautiful flower.

The techniques described herein are not the only ones suitable for *phalaenopsis* culture, but they work well for me and can also work well for you.

The phalaenopsis is not only the most beautiful flower in the plant kingdom, but also one of the easiest to grow and enjoy. What the African violet *(saintpaulia)* was to the late '40s and early '50s, the phalaenopsis is and will be to the late '80s and early '90s. It already shows signs of exceeding the popularity of the African violet, probably because all those violet growers are finding the phalaenopsis is the next logical step up the ladder of beauty, sophistication, and challenge.

The parallel continues: If you can grow and flower African violets, phals are a piece of cake. Culture is a bit more complex, but not much...and the flowers are enormously more gratifying. IF YOU CAN HANDLE AFRICAN VIOLETS, YOU WILL HAVE NO DIFFICULTY WITH PHALAENOPSIS.

Phalaenopsis blooms come on spikes ranging anywhere from 1 inch to 48 inches long; in all colors from pristine white to a red-lavender so dark it approaches black. (No, there isn't a real black orchid...yet); in sizes from 1/2-inch to 5 inches; and in sizes and colors perfect for personal adornment for anything from a boutonniere to a bridal bouquet.

Some phals have an incredibly beautiful fragrance. It's different from any I've ever sensed; a cool, exquisite perfume that seems to come from everywhere at once...in the evening, usually. If you're into exotic fragrances, select your plants for that quality. There aren't many, but those that are fragrant are worth the effort to find them.

THE PHALS CAN BE GROWN **IN CULTIVATION** ANYWHERE FROM AS FAR NORTH AS NORTHERN CANADA TO AS FAR SOUTH AS THE SOUTHERN TIP OF SOUTH AMERICA.

Mature plants bloom for periods ranging from 1 to as long as 3 months...and can do that twice each year.

And they're houseplants.

And you can grow them.

Now.

How? Read on.

Welcome to the world of the elegant phalaenopsis orchid.

(Many thanks to my good friends John Neidhamer and Dr. Bob Engel for their constructive criticisms of this work in draft. Blame for any shortcomings of the book can now be shared among the three of us. Thanks, guys. B.G.)

SECTION 1. BEFORE WE START

1.1 HOUSEPLANTS

Up front, I'd like you to know that phalaenopsis orchids are houseplants; they're houseplants in the same sense that African violets are.

Phals qualify as houseplants because they like the same conditions that we like in our homes...soft light, warm temperatures, and slightly moist air. When we're comfortable, so are they.

They are not fragile exotics that are grown by really weird people using magic stuff or anything like that. And they don't grow only in Hawaii. They can be grown and flowered right here, wherever you're reading this.

Phalaenopsis are houseplants grown by ordinary people who like flowers. You'd be amazed to see how ordinary the very best growers really are. The only thing extra-ordinary about them is the plant they grow...and it is magnificent.

It's important at the outset that you understand the phalaenopsis (or phal for short) is not an exotic guest in your home, but rather a lovely friend you'll like having around. It's important that you recognize this early on because otherwise you'll be afraid of them and there isn't much point in having a friend you are afraid of.

Regarding the African violets, if you have had any success at all in growing them, you will have little trouble in growing phalaenopsis. Their cultures are very similar, but with a few important exceptions.

One of those exceptions is light and it is a very important difference. Phals will not flower in a north window as will the violets. They will vegetate, but won't flower. More on those details a bit later.

1.2 A GREENHOUSE?

You probably are getting the message that **a greenhouse is not necessary for growing phals.** You're right. There are advantages to having a greenhouse for them, but it is not necessary if you have only a small number of plants, say up to 25. The break point comes when you get tired of carrying plants to the sink to water them. I've known people who have patiently carried 50-75 plants to the sink twice a week, but I don't recommend it.

The point is that if you don't have a greenhouse or any prospects of getting one, you will have to limit the number of plants you grow to the number you are willing to tote back and forth from the sink. You can have a lot of enjoyment from the plants up to that number.

Many of us are hung up on having some of everything that looks good, but our reasoning for doing that gets a little fuzzy. If you are growing a limit of 25 phals and another one shows up that you can't do without, it just means you have to get rid of one...a good idea when you see the load of mediocrity many of us are carrying. Build a greenhouse when quantity becomes as important as quality and not before.

There *are* alternatives to having a greenhouse to house your phals and we will talk about them a bit later on.

1.3 WHAT TO START WITH?

When you buy your first 10 phals, get the cheap ones. These are your 'practice plants' and they stand a good chance of becoming sacrificial lambs on the altar of orchid learning. Every phal grower loses *some* plants and a measure of experience in the game is the number you've guided to the big nursery in the sky. One goal of this book is to hold that number down to affordable size.

Later, you can step right up with the big guys and buy an unbloomed beauty with the conviction that it will last at least until the canceled check comes back. Don't try to hurry that day. Remember telling your kids something like that? Same point. It is not easy to maintain a cool head when you get orchid fever...and you are tempted to mortgage the grandkids' education for that tall, serene pink beauty you can't do without. But do it.

Don't buy unbloomed seedlings at least for the first year. They have some special needs that can complicate your learning process. Buy mature, blooming plants only at first.

This is not to say that you should avoid seedlings permanently, only until you are able to handle basic needs of the mature plants. Then, take on seedlings.

An unflowered seedling offers the intrigue of the unknown. No one knows what the flower will look like until it flowers. So amateurs and professionals, alike, have the same chance of drawing a winner.

This 'chance' is a significant event with phals, because the variety of outcomes of a hybrid cross can be wide. It's like buying a lottery ticket. You could be a BIG WINNER. When you go out in the morning and see some brave, new little face looking back up at you with the innocence and joy of first bloom, you get a little closer to the meaning of life. At that time, only you and the Good Lord know what that flower looks like. That will renew your faith and get tired juices flowing again. Wow!

Buy the cheapies at the outset and allow plenty of time for your personal development. This is a hobby that will probably keep you fascinated for the rest of your life, so slow down, OK? *Now* is the time to stop and smell the flowers.

1.4 HOW TO BUY PHAL PLANTS

Ask at local nurseries and if they don't have them, ask for recommendations. Ask if there are orchid growers in your area. Established hobbyists are an excellent source since upgrading-your-collection is a game all of us play and almost all collections are bulging at the greenhouse walls with surplus plants.

Write for plant lists from the sources with asterisks after their names in Section 8.4 of this book. There are others besides the few listed there, but I know and respect these folks.

Go to visit a phal nursery...if possible betweeen January and June in the northern hemisphere. That's prime blooming season.

Watch for orchid flower shows. Visit and meet with growers and they will most likely help you find local sources of plants and supplies.

If you are traveling on business or pleasure, try to include orchid stops along the way. I traveled on business extensively during my early orchid years and met a lot of interesting people from whom I've learned much of what is in print here. There is a direct correlation between the number of phal people you talk to and how much you learn.

1.5 SPECIES OR HYBRIDS?

A point to remember when selecting phal plants, if you have any choice in the matter, is the species or wild forms are usually tougher and more reliable bloomers than the complex hybrids.

Same for the primary crosses, those made with two species. These are your best bet for openers. They are tolerant of bizarre culture and are all-around reliable performers. (You can recognize species plants by the name on the plant tag...it starts with a lower case letter. Hybrid names begin with capitals.)

Unfortunately, species and primary hybrids are also the plain-Janes of the phal world. They are not the extravagant spectaculars you see among the hybrids, but they have many devoted fans.

1.6 AND...

One last point: Please try to be tolerant with the less fortunate, innocent growers of the other flowers and other genera of orchids in your relationships with them. Maybe some day they'll see the light and grow phals, too.

So, when you're telling them how great it is to be a phal grower, try not to be too superior. It's lonely up here for us phal growers.

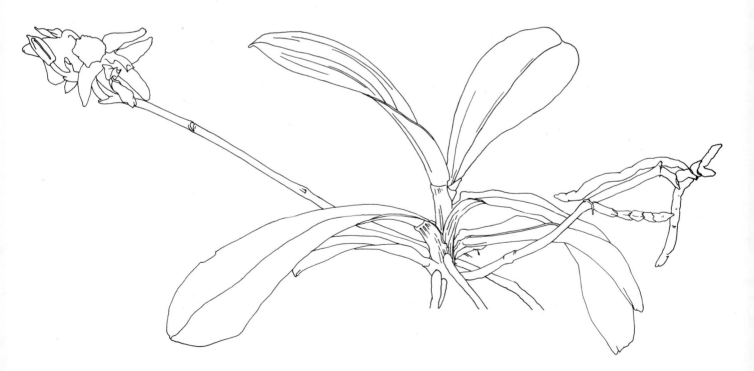

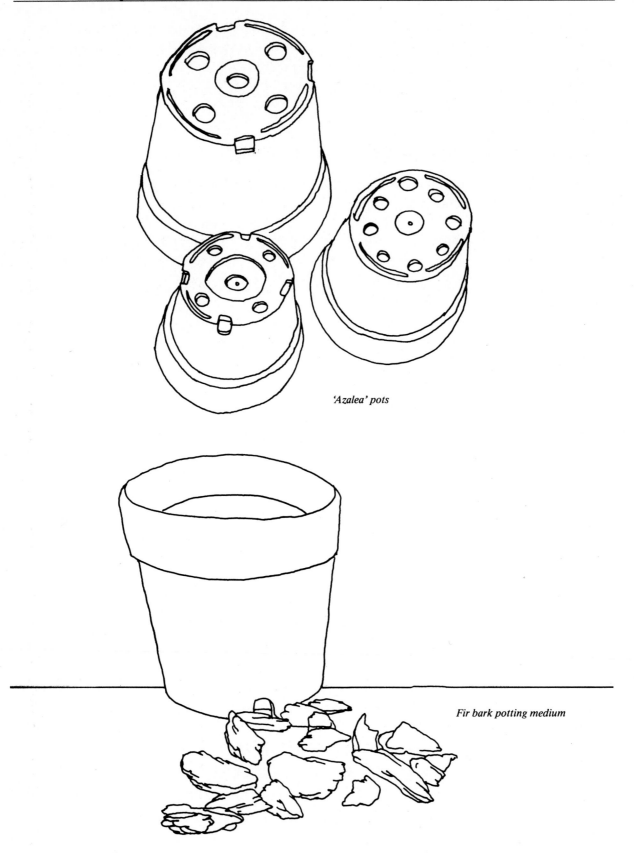

'Azalea' pots

Fir bark potting medium

SECTION 2. IN THE BEGINNING

2.1 GENERAL CULTURAL NEEDS:

LIGHT:
They like 15% of full sunlight in autumn and 10% the rest of the year. You have about 15% of full sunlight when a fuzzy shadow is barely discernible as you hold one hand 8 inches above the other. You have about 10% when the same shadow is not quite discernible. Phals need direct, but filtered sunlight. Northern sky light will not do.

TEMPERATURE:
Give them 60° at night to preferably not over 85°F. in the day throughout the year, except 3 weeks in early autumn when nighttime minimums should be lowered to 55°.

WATER:
Do not allow plants to dry out. Keep potting medium moist, no matter what your cattleya-growing friends say. Water from the top of the pot only. Allow water to run through the medium for several seconds to saturate it, then set the plant aside to drain.

POTTING MEDIUM:
For mature plants, use quarter- to half-inch pieces of fir bark that is available through most gardening outlets. Use tree fern in the Southeastern US. Avoid large, hard barks that are slow to absorb water.

Seedling bark mix (eighth- to quarter-inch) is satisfactory for plants up to blooming size.

This is not to imply these are the only suitable potting materials for phals. I use them because they are available and cheap.

Check for locally-available materials if fir bark is not at hand.

DRAINAGE:
Four-inch pots should have drainage holes with at least one square inch in area. Six-inch pots should have at least two square inches of drainage holes. Good drainage is essential to plant health. Don't assume drainage is OK. It usually isn't.

AIR MOVEMENT:
In a greenhouse, provide gentle air movement constantly; increase velocity on hot days and cold nights. In the home no additional air circulation is needed.

These are the conditions your new phals would like to enjoy. Some straying from these values isn't going to hurt anything, but it *is* important to stay close.

Let this first page of suggestions settle for a bit before we go on. Get comfortable with these ideas and then we'll be a little more specific.

2.2 SPECIFIC CULTURAL NEEDS:

LIGHT:
Phals like direct, but filtered sunlight. One-tenth of full sunlight or about 1000 footcandles is what they like best throughout most of the year. This is easy to obtain in a south or east window that has a lace curtain, a roll-up blind or a tree outside to reduce the light to the 'dappled' level. 'Bright shade', if that helps any.

More than that will bleach or even sunburn the leaves. If your leaves are a medium green, you are right about where you should be. You may wonder how they can tolerate the bright sunlight in the trees of the southwest Pacific if they are so sensitive to light.

The answer is moving air and moving tree branches. Keep a breeze blowing over them and they will tolerate much higher light levels because the moving air keeps the leaves cool.

For what it's worth, **too little light is the most common cause of phalaenopsis plants not blooming.** Direct light means just that...in the direct rays of the sun; but *filtered* to hold down the light level and leaf temperatures.

TEMPERATURES:

This one is easy. If you're comfortable, the plant will be, too. Minimum temperature is 60 degrees F. and maximum is about 85 degrees F. Five degrees over or under won't do the plant any harm, but growth may be retarded during that time. Other problems pop up during over- and under-temperatures, too.

WATER AND FEEDING:

Phals like to have their roots damp, but not wet. Does that make any sense? In the summer that means watering about twice a week and about once a week in the winter. More on this later.

Fertilize them with every watering. Use about 1/4 the strength called for on the package of whatever fertilizer you have on hand. Later on you may want to use special fertilizers, but at this stage any kind will do. Water 'occasionally' with just plain water to flush the pots of old fertilizer salts.

HUMIDITY:

The phals grow naturally in areas of high humidity, so that is a condition we must try to duplicate. High levels of humidity are not common in much of the US or in heated/air-conditioned homes anywhere. Humidity is easy to create in those situations, though, by putting the plant on a tray of wet gravel, an inch or two deep. Add water daily to keep up with evaporation losses and don't let the pot sit in water. As an article of faith, please accept that constantly wet roots can cause rot problems.

REPOTTING:

Phals should be repotted or 'transplanted' about every 2 years or when the potting medium or 'soil' has broken down to the point where you can push your index finger down into it. The bark we're using to support the plant is vegetable matter which will rot eventually and collapse...unlike sandy soil which does not.

Make an entry of when it was done on the plant tag to avoid confusion in the future...e.g. "Rep 7/19/86".

AIR MOVEMENT:

Gentle air movement makes the plant feel good and helps prevent disease. It also holds down leaf surface temperatures if the light gets too bright and this can prevent sunburn.

That's it. And you, too, can grow the serenely beautiful 'moth orchid'. It's worth knowing that most adolescent phals will have half again as many flowers which are a third larger in the second and subsequent years. You probably bought one that is blooming for the first time, so rest easy; the best is yet to come. ✿

SECTION 3. AFTER A LITTLE PRACTICE

Y ou are ready for this section when you feel comfortable with your orchids and are over the initial fear that those expensive little boogers are going to turn up their toes and embarrass you right there in front of everybody. You're past the big hurdle keeping them alive and ready for phase II, ensuring they bloom.

By now you probably are aware that, given the basic conditions called for in the previous section, there is little you can do, short of hitting themwith a stick, to <u>keep</u> them from blooming. They have gotten along nicely for millions of years in the wild without your or my ministrations, so there's little reason to expect things to change.

3.1 TEMPERATURE

We're going to continue to maintain a 60-85°F. range, but modify it just a little to fine-tune temperatures to the plant's needs. We're going to try to duplicate the environment the plant would enjoy in the wild; even in the tropics the temperature will vary from season to season.

COOL AIR SOAK TRICK ...
It takes a period of cooler than normal nights to "set" the flower spikes. This is true of many flowering plants.

In the early fall when nighttime temperatures fall below 60°F., **PUT THE PLANTS OUTSIDE FOR 3 WEEKS.** Not in the full sun, but "outside" enough so they see low temperatures between 55-58°F. at night. They need to be chilled for that long to guarantee

that they will flower when the season arrives. They *may* bloom anyway, but it doesn't take much effort to *ensure* that they do.

This fall chilling is the reason for the warning in the previous section about nighttime temps that are too high. There are other reasons for needing cool night temperatures, but overly-warm nights may *prevent* flowering of the plant. When you know this cool air soak trick, you can count yourself ahead of 90% of all orchid growers.

One more time, chill your phals at night in the fall down to 55°F. for 3 weeks, then go back to normal growing conditions.

If you live in cold country, setting the thermostat down to 55° at night will have the desired effect. It won't hurt to chill them to 55° for more than 3 weeks, but do so no later than the first of December (June in the southern hemisphere). Then raise the minimum nighttime temperature to 60-62 degrees ... and hold that until the plant blooms.

3.2 LIGHT

A guess at the intensity of the light falling on your phals is usually good enough to ensure flowering, but an accurate measurement is much better. If you have a light intensity meter, terrific. If not, don't worry, your plants will tell you all about it.

You can tell if your phals are not getting enough light by: (1) they won't flower; and (2) the leaves will be soft and of a dark, green color. Move them to a brighter spot.

You can tell if they are getting too much light by: (1) the leaves will be light green-yellow in color; and (2) the blooms will be small, hard and may even stick closed. You may also see some leaf tissue turn brown on the "recurve" surface of the leaf where it bends in the middle and down. The sunburned tissue is dead, but the problem will not spread. The answer to the over-light condition, of course, is to increase the shading a bit.

Make adjustments in light level and temperature in small increments. Don't make big changes in a short time. Give the plant a chance to adjust. Slow and easy does it. Just like people.

At the same time you're putting the plants outside in the fall to lower the nighttime temperatures, try to increase the amount of light they get for that same period of time. A 50% increase in light to 1500 footcandles during the fall chilling period will aid in setting flower spikes.

As is the case with any orchid, when you increase the amount of light it receives you should increase the air circulation to keep the leaves cool during sunny periods.

Try to give the phals at least 6 hours of daylight each day in the spring and fall. The other seasons will average out just fine.

Growing phals under lights is a popular way of enjoying them in cooler areas where sunlight in the winter months may not be enough to make them bloom. There is some excellent literature available on this and other orchid subjects from the following sources:

Twin Oaks Books
4343 Causeway Dr
Lowell, MI 49331

and the

American Orchid Society
6000 So. Olive Ave
West Palm Beach, FL 33405

3.3 WATERING AND FEEDING

Phalaenopsis orchids don't have the same needs for fertilizer throughout all the seasons of the year. . .and trying to figure what they need and at which times gets bit confusing. Then the real problem arises: How to keep track of what you've done and when you did it. The Answer: Feed them with every watering throughout the year and your scheduling problem is solved.

Best approach is to use one-quarter of the strength fertilizer recommended on the package of whatever you're using ... and get into the habit of feeding with every watering. If you miss a few and use just plain water, you're still in good shape. The plants won't miss an occasional meal.

Phals do not like their roots to be too dry.

Do not let the potting medium ('soil', until you get comfortable with the correct term 'medium') dry out. Don't worry, they aren't going to go belly-up if they get a tad dry, but make a practice of keeping the medium a little moist. I didn't say wet, just moist. **This is not a recommendation to water every other day to show your plants how much you love them!**

If you prefer numbers to work with instead of a principle, try this watering schedule:

Warm, dry days	3 days
Cool, dry days	4 days
Warm, moist days	5 days
Cool, moist days	10 days

This probably won't cover all situations, but it will get you started.

Very cold water on phals can damage leaves and flower buds.

Tap water in colder areas can drop down into the 40's in the winter and, at that temperature, is not suitable for use on the phals. If your tap water drops below 60°F. in the winter, draw the water the day before using and let it stand at room temperature overnight.

In any event, it's prudent to keep water off the leaves and, especially, off the flower spikes during the watering process in the winter. The buds are most susceptible to thermal damage when they are just forming and are still soft. The use of tepid water is an insurance measure...and highly recommended.

Any houseplant fertilizer will do in the beginning. If you are fertilizer-literate, use a balanced ratio...of 18-18-18 or 20-20-20. Otherwise, anything from fish emulsion to African violet food will do. Caution: Use fish emulsion only in the summer...when the windows are open. Whew!

Your avante-garde grower-friends may try to sell you on the latest gardener's darling, but stick to the basics.

Don't apply a fertilizer solution to a dry plant. If a plant is very dry, water it now and fertilize tomorrow. A salty fertilizer solution can be harmful to a desiccated plant. The usual tell-tale sign is blackened leaf tips.

When in doubt, do without.

3.4 HUMIDITY

Surprisingly, humidity is not much of a problem with phals for home growers. It only becomes a factor in cultivation of the orchids when they are grown in very dry conditions and even then it's not always a problem. In the desert or anywhere refrigerated air-conditioning is used, passable humidity can be maintained for phals by placing the plant on a shallow tray of gravel kept wet. Phals aren't too happy in refrigerated air-conditioning, but they will tolerate it.

If your plants seem to dry out faster then you might expect, or if flower buds sometimes stick closed...try increasing the humidity by the tray of gravel method above. In dry areas where evaporative coolers are used, you have the problem solved. Watch for leaf limpness, though, and shorten the watering interval during the heat of the summer.

Orchids get along famously with evaporative or 'swamp coolers'. But they get along with refrigerated air-conditioning about as well as cats get along with vacuum cleaners. They don't. The air is too dry. (Aside: I haven't had a summer cold since we shut off our central air-conditioning 10 years ago and began using a 'swamp cooler'. Living with plants requires some adjustments.)

3.5 AIR MOVEMENT

Moving air is essential to the health of phals. Not much is needed and it isn't a problem for in-home growers. But, if you have your plants in a brighter-than-recommended spot, point a little fan at them and leave it on...period. The little 'personal' or desk fans usually cost under $10 and will do just fine on low speed.

STILL AIR IS BAD NEWS FOR ANY ORCHID.

You don't have to look far for the reason why: Air moves constantly in the trees where the orchids grow in nature. The moving air keeps them cool and dries them off quickly after a rain. Dry leaves are usually free of bacterial and fungal problems.

If you have a ceiling fan in the room with your plants, turn it on 'low' and leave it on. Your plants will bless you.

3.6 POTTING AND POTTING MEDIA

Generally speaking, mature phals should be repotted every 2 years.

Repot (1) when the medium is broken down; (2) when the plant has outgrown the pot; and (3) any time the plant looks less than robust.

Look at the stuff in the pot that's holding the plant up ('medium') and dig down a little and get some between your thumb and forefinger. Pinch it. If it feels firm and resists crumbling, it probably is in fairly good condition. If it crumbles a little, it's in fair condition. If it smears, you need to repot now.

If it's in good condition, follow the schedule on section 3.3. If it's only in fair condition, lengthen the interval between waterings by 2 days.

3.7 REPOTTING

To repot a phalaenopsis, pull the plant out of the pot and pick the old medium from the roots. Wash the dirt off the roots in tepid running water. Flame a pair of scissors or shears lightly in a propane or alcohol torch,

then trim off the dead roots. A kitchen gas burner will do just fine, but just pass the blades through slowly. Single-edged razor blades or inexpensive, all-metal steak knives can be batch-sterilized in the oven at 450°F. for 15 minutes. They will work almost as well as shears.

Hold the plant roots centered in the pot with the top root about an inch below the lip of the pot. With your other hand, pour in the bark ('Pathway' size; it meets the size requirements mentioned earlier and is readily available) or tree fern to fill all the voids between the roots. Tap the pot firmly to settle everything and add a bit more medium to bring the level up to about 1 inch below the rim. Keep track of the date repotted on the plant tag.

Some growers repot on a regular schedule...most of us.

If you don't want to do your own, some nurseries and many hobbyists will do it for you for a modest fee.

Use the finger-in-the-medium method whenever you suspect something is wrong. Sometimes a bad batch of bark or tree fern will break down before the 2 years runs out. When that happens, the roots will suffer and so will the plant. So *any time a plant looks puny, suspect the medium is bad...and change it. Can't hurt.* You feel better with clean socks, don't you?

OK, that's a broad brush on what has to be done to grow your phalaenopsis orchids. Now let's take a look at when to do it.

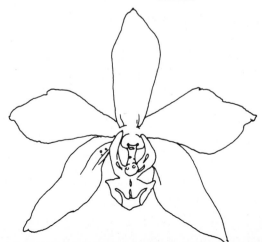

SECTION 4. REGULAR CARE THEY NEED

4.1 DAILY CARE

1. Look at and enjoy them. Contemplate nature's most complex, most highly evolved...and most exquisite flower.

2. Watch for abrupt changes in growth. This habit will help you detect possible problems.

3. Note the progress of growth and anticipate flowering in season. (Note: This is not just a dumb blandishment. It is the reason for growing these beauties. **Have at it and piddle away all the time you can afford and don't feel guilty about it.** Someone said the hours spent in contemplation of nature's grandeur don't count against the total the Good Lord allows us on earth. Hear, hear.)

4. Observe a watering and feeding interval of 4-5 days in the summer and 8-10 days in the winter. If you live in a dry climate, shorten the interval a tad. If you live in a moist climate, lengthen it a little.

5. Watch for the arrival of bugs and other wildlife on the plants. Refer to Section 7 if something shows up that you don't recognize or particularly want on your plants. Exception: Cats and grandchildren. You're on your own with them.

6. Watch for diseases which can affect both mature and immature phals...and there are some.

(Note that I put all the unpleasant stuff in one section to get it over with and avoid blackening the whole book with gloom and doom. See Section 7 for what to do about those problems.)

7. Pick off dead leaves and flowers.

8. Take a look at the weekly, monthly and seasonal special care items to see if any are due.

4.2 WEEKLY CARE

1. Check to see if the changing season is appreciably changing the amount of light or heat the plants get. The sun angle changes and this can cause some distress to the plants. Adjust as necessary.

2. Check the calendar you made last year of the arrival times of local insect pests. (More on this in Section 7.) If they arrived last year in this month, use an insecticide on the plants to greet the wretched, little beasts when they arrive. And keep on using it until their local season is past. Of course, use as the label directs. Don't fudge on those directions. Use pesticides with great care, the same way you would with any medication for any other member of your family.

4.3 MONTHLY CARE

1. Check the **Seasonal Care** schedules and the annual care program on page 19 for upcoming special needs.

2. Review **Weekly** and **Daily Care** schedules to see if anything has been overlooked.

4.4 SPRING CARE

1. Increase the shading plants get as days get longer and the sun gets brighter.

2. Stake flower spikes to keep the long ones upright and showing the flowers to their best advantage. Tie the flower spike to a wire or bamboo stake just below the first bud and do that before the flower opens. Flower spike 'carriage' will be much better with that little bit of help. Nature didn't have human sensitivities in mind when she developed the flower spike...only propagation of the species. She was trying to please a bug, not us.

3. Look to shortening the watering interval as temps rise and days lengthen.

4.5 FALL CARE

1. Increase the light the plants get to about 50% more than throughout the rest of the year. This will help set flower spikes for the spring bloomers...which includes most phalaenopsis. Reduce the light to normal about the first of December (northern hemisphere).

2. Chill the plants with nighttime temps down to 55°F. or so. Don't get carried away. They are tropical plants. Chill nightly for 3 weeks, then return to normal indoor temperatures.

3. If you are fertilizer literate, use a high-phosphorous food during the fall months. Hi-phos is the mix where the middle number of the ratios is the largest of the three. If you are one of the vast majority who is not at home with fertilizer ratios, don't worry about it. The motive for this one is enrichment and this is not an essential.

4. Do whatever potting is needed during September; in March, Down Under.

5. Cut any flower spikes remaining back to the bottom during the same time as 4. above...even if they still have blooms. Put those spikes in a bud vase and enjoy them for another several weeks. **DON'T SKIP THIS STEP.** The plants need rest to get ready for the next blooming season. The flower spike is a burden to the plant and it can't rest until it is removed. If it dies off on its own, fine. If not, remove it. Did you hear me?

6. Get ready for the Big Show...which usually starts in January in the northern hemisphere; July, down under.

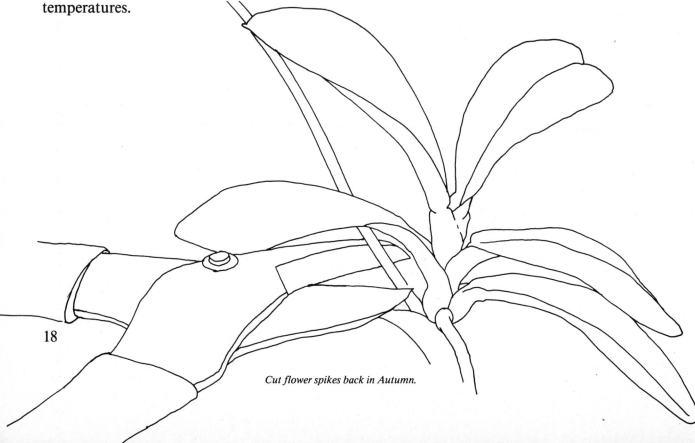

Cut flower spikes back in Autumn.

4.6 ANNUAL PROGRAM...A QUICK LOOK
(Northern Hemisphere)

* JANUARY....... Here come the flowers!

* FEBRUARY ..... Increase shading; stake flower spikes.

* MARCH .... Water more often, now. Watch for orchid shows.

* APRIL .... Just enjoy. More shows. Dazzle the folks at the office by taking in a flowering phal.

* MAY .... Watch for arrival of mites. Go get 'em.

** JUNE .... Summer spikes and *violacea-amboinensis* species.

** JULY .... Watch for signs of too much light and too little water. Adjust each as necessary.

** AUGUST .... About Labor Day (the first week in September), cut flower spikes back. Go ahead, do it...I <u>know</u> you don't want to, but...

SEPTEMBER ... Start increasing light; repot as necessary; back off a bit on watering.

OCTOBER ...... Cool soak plants; feed with high phosphorous fertilizer this month (optional).

NOVEMBER .... Thanksgiving and snail time.

DECEMBER .... Sit and wait...maybe someone will give you an orchid or an orchid book for Christmas or Hanukkah.

* = Spring flowering season.
** = Summer flowering season.

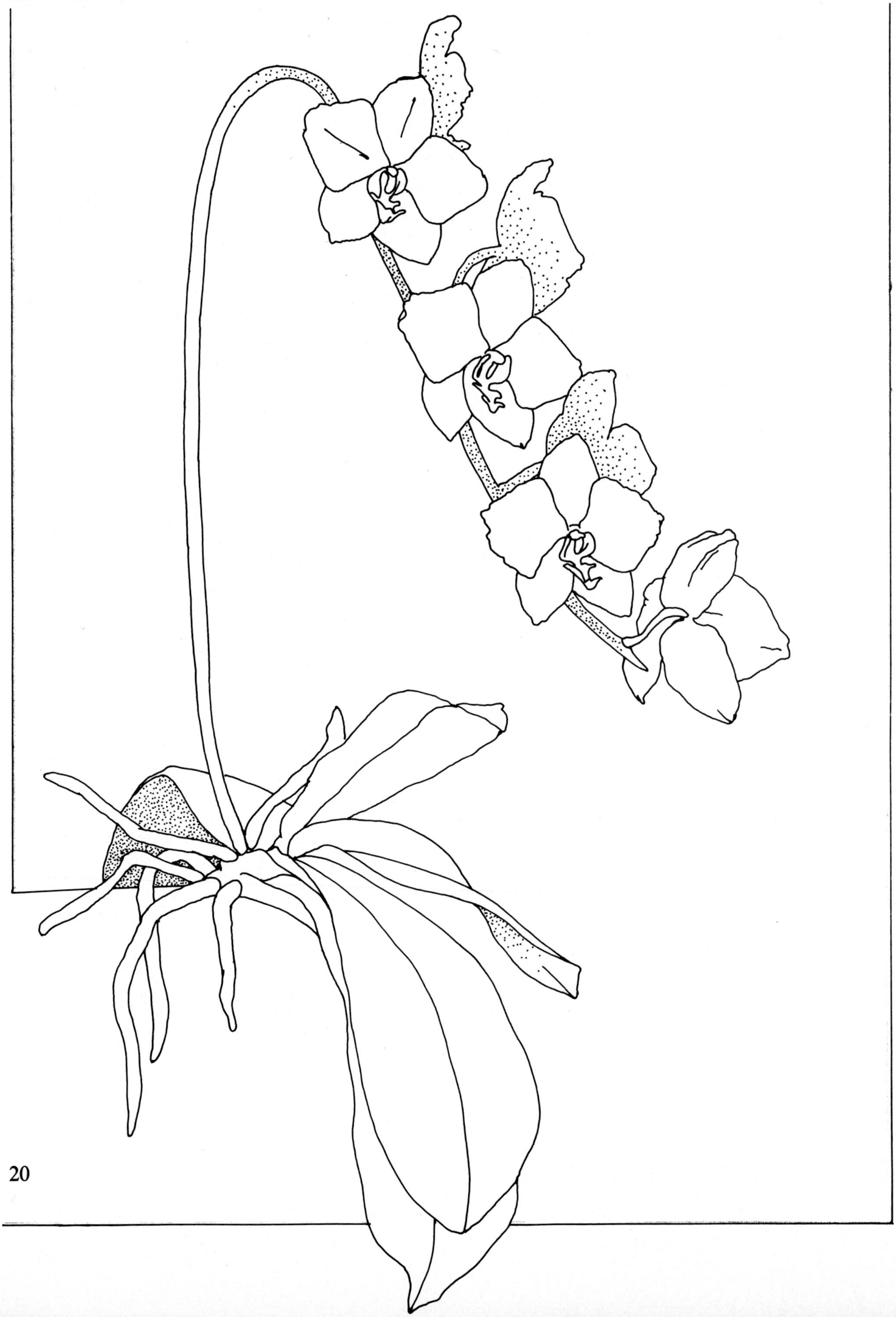

SECTION 5. WHERE TO GROW THEM

5.1 HOUSE VS GREENHOUSE

If you have a greenhouse, your problem of where to grow them is solved.

If not, it may take a little imagination and an appreciation of what the plants need. There is no magic formula that says 'bathrooms are good and bedrooms are not'. Each potential location has to be judged on its merits regarding light, temperature, accessibility, attractiveness and suitability in your home scheme of things.

Whether you can water the plants in-place is going to loom large as a consideration as the size of your collection grows. . .because there is a limit on how many plants you are going to be willing to lug to the sink for watering. The real problem is that the nuisance of moving plants to the sink may encourage you to let the watering schedule slide and the plants will suffer. . .and not give you their best.

To further complicate matters, weather and the season can affect how well a phal does in any given location. . .it could be fine in the summer and unsatisfactory in the winter. It may be necessary to move them about seasonally. Many people move them during changes of season to keep growing conditions peaked.

But, barring the building of a greenhouse you will have to work with what your living space provides, so let's look at some possibilities.

5.2 DIRECTIONS

First, if you don't know where the *cardinal points or directions* are from known reference points around the house, FIND THEM. You'll need to know where north, east, south and west are. We can't proceed until you have a handle on this. Tie a geographical feature to each direction and it will be a little easier.

The Hawaiians call north 'windward', south 'leeward', east 'Diamond Head' and west 'Ewa' (Beach). Very handy if you're standing in downtown Honolulu, but a little confusing if you're anywhere else. . .but it works.

If directions confuse you try relating east to things like 'pool', west to 'garage', and so on. Locally, north is 'the mountains', but, for our needs here, it is important to find how your living quarters are situated with regard to the compass.

Try rhyming suggestive words as navigators do in remembering magnetic compass corrections: ''East is least and West is best.'' Make up your own.

It's hard to find south if you don't know where to look for it.

OK, now that you know where you are (and everybody has to be <u>somewhere</u>), here are the ratings of directions as they suit phals:

South. Terrific. If you can find a spot with a southern exposure, terrific, you're in tall cotton. Absolutely the best in terms of light and temperature.

East. Good, because you get the light without heat. One catch, though. The phals need about 6 hours of sunlight each day in the fall and spring (winter and summer will take care of themselves). Southeast is better because the 6-hour problem is solved. (Southeast is midway between south and east.)

West. OK. If you can't find a spot with a southern or eastern exposure, west will do. It may get a bit warm, though, so watch your plants for signs of too much heat and light, particularly in summer.

North. Forget it. No orchids I know of will bloom with only a northern exposure. Reason? They need <u>direct</u> or reflected sunlight; northern sky light only won't do.

NOTE: REVERSE NORTH AND SOUTH IN THE SOUTHERN HEMISPHERE.

One other direction to consider is overhead. And that is absolutely the best you can get. That's why greenhouses are so perfect; they match nature. Either a solarium or an atrium with a skylight is very good and every bit as good as a greenhouse. Do you have a skylight? That will take care of a few plants and keep them right out where you can see them.

You can control the amount of light the plants receive by raising them toward the skylight to increase it and lowering them to decrease.

5.3 FINDING THE RIGHT PLACE

Finding the right place to grow your phals is important. If you have the wrong spot, nothing you can do will <u>make</u> them bloom. If you have the right spot, nothing you can do will <u>keep</u> them from blooming...well, almost nothing.

Do you have a 'bright spot' in the house? Super, start your search for a growing spot there. If there is too much light, you can always cut it down with something. But going from dark to light is another matter ...without lights.

Sometimes sunlight bouncing off a light-colored wall will provide just the right amount of light. A dark wall painted a light color can transform a losing spot to a winner. Reflected light is OK, but north sky light is not. The only light coming from the north sky is sunlight reflecting off pollutants in the atmosphere and that just isn't enough.

A temporary fix might be a reflector made of a piece of plywood covered with crinkled aluminum foil. The movie industry has used them for years.

A windowsill.
The classic houseplant location. We want 'dappled' sunlight, we don't want the plant to bake, and we'd like a little moving air, please. A southern window is best, but others will do. If you find a candidate, increase the shade some before trusting your pretty to the hot sun. Hang a little shade cloth, some cheese cloth, a lace curtain, or any such screen to full sun at first.

Give it more shade than you think it needs...for starters. You can increase the light if it's not enough, but the consequences of too much light are more drastic.

Windowsills usually don't enjoy moving air unless the window is opened a little or a small fan used. Keep in mind that more light has to be matched with more air movement to keep the plant cool.

In the winter windowsills often get unacceptably cool at night, even in warm country. Either remove the plant from the windowsills at night or draw blinds to keep the cold drafts off them.

An extended windowsill.

Windowsill growing area can be doubled or tripled by adding a board supported by shelf brackets. This is the cheapest way to expand your growing space.

Greenhouse- or Garden-Windows.

The all-glass bay windows, which have come back into vogue in recent years, are good for phal culture if a few precautions are taken. Get the kind with clear glass instead of the smoked or bronze-tinted. The tinting is a selective filter and the part of sunlight which is filtered out may be important to growth and flowering. If you already have a tinted window, try it anyway. It may work.

Get one with vents. They get pretty hot and ventilation is essential. If you have no vents in the window, keep a fan going on the plants constantly. Good idea under <u>any</u> circumstances.

The earlier counsel on shading applies here, too. **Shading is essential on garden-windows.** Keep an eye open for the need for extra watering during the early weeks of use of this kind of growing location and during bright, hot weather.

Plant carts

A plant cart is an extended windowsill, too...one that can be moved <u>to</u> the window for more heat and light, or one that can be moved <u>from</u> the window for the opposite effect. It has the added advantage of providing a means of transport for the plants between the growing spot and the watering hole.

An old tea cart, or even a new one is a good start. (Look out, garage sale; here I come!) A more durable, but less decorative, setup would start with one of those two decked pushcarts used in restaurants to carry soiled dishes to the washroom.

With this kind of a start, it's an easy step to equipping the cart with lights, a plastic coverlet (as in birdcage or teapot, but bigger) to keep things moist, warm and protected from drafts at night. Beats having company come into your bathroom to admire the flowers. Wheel it out instead. This is a very popular arrangement with the artificial light growers.

If you are really handy at these things, enclose it with glass instead of plastic, put an electric heating cable on the bottom and a fan inside and you have the ultimate. Take the wheels off and you have what the early orchid hunters in the mid-1800's called a Wardian Case.

But why take the wheels off? They make your mobile windowsill functional and simplify all of your maintenance chores.

There are some terrific drawings, photos and ideas on this subject in Rebecca Tyson Northen's book *Orchids As House Plants*, Dover Publications, New York; ISBN 0-486-23261-1.

Bathrooms.

Bathrooms are fine, so long as the other needs are met. The added humidity in bathrooms is largely an illusion...unless water is running constantly and even then there's no great advantage. An extended shelf in the bathroom will work just fine. Small windows used in bathrooms are something of a disadvantage, though. OK for a couple of plants, but that's about it.

Kitchens.

One caution: If you have gas appliances in the kitchen and their combustion is not complete, flowers will wilt quickly. An incorrectly adjusted gas flame can cause the release of ethylene or a similar gas, that can shorten phal flower lives to a matter of just a few hours...or less. Overly ripe apples, bananas or similar sweet fruits can have the same effect. Recall the old adage about one rotten apple spoiling the whole barrel? Ethylene gas.

Enclosed Porches or Solariums.

These bright, airy porches are the transition between indoors and outdoors. As such they have some qualities of each, and can be an excellent alternative to a greenhouse...or an expedient until you get one.

All the previous comments apply here as well, plus an additional problem of the difference between day and nighttime temperatures. Most of these porches are not heated, so they are suitable only so long as nighttime temps stay within an acceptable range.

In dry country watch daytime humidity levels. Phals will desiccate in a matter of days on an open or screened porch. **Open or screened porches in the dry areas are not recommended any time of the year for phals.** The humidity just isn't there and can't be maintained without expensive equipment.

Outdoors.

'Summering out' is feasible in most parts of the temperate zone and any country where humidity stays above 35% relative humidity and temperatures range between 60 and 85°F. Phals will tolerate slightly higher light levels outdoors than indoors because of the increase in air movement.

If phals are summered out, even in a lath house, take care to ensure they are under cover. Afternoon or evening rains can leave water in the crowns of the plants and could lead to crown rot, the original phalaenopsis bad news.

This warning applies to tropical areas such as south Florida, Hawaii, Puerto Rico, USVI, islands of the Caribbean and the southwest Pacific and northern Australia. In nature, they don't suffer the problem, because their skins are tougher from constant exposure to the sun and because their locations, well up in the trees, lead to rapid drying.

One last problem with growing phals outdoors in built-up areas: Smog. Even heavy smog usually won't threaten the life of a phalaenopsis plant, but it will absolutely destroy the blooms, buds and seed capsules. Evaporative coolers are useful in this regard in that they will wash a lot of the crud out of the air. Wags note that Southern Californians are not happy unless they can *see* what they are breathing...but the phals can do without smog, nicely, thank you.

Some phals are sensitive to smog to the extent that they can't be grown in areas where smog concentrations are high. The first indication is loss of buds and flowers.

Unfortunately, the only way you can learn which ones are affected is by trying them. Some orchid nurseries like Stewart Orchids in San Gabriel, California, have done a lot of work in developing smog-resistant varieties. If smog is a problem, get in touch with:

Stewart Orchids
P. O. Box 307
San Gabriel, CA 91778

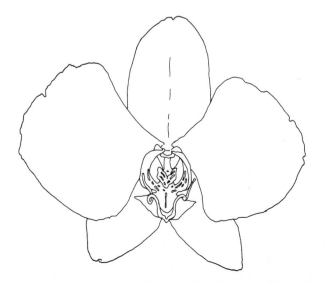

SECTION 6. SHOWING THEM OFF

THERE IS NO JOY IN HAVING SOMETHING BEAUTIFUL IF YOU CAN'T SHARE IT WITH OTHERS.

This little bit of philosophy is the driving force behind many of our human endeavors, including, for many, orchid growing.

Finding new ways to show them in the home and outside it is a delight for many of us. And there is a higher calling for all orchid growers, if they can stand the tariff . . . _giving_ them away.

You'll have about as much trouble giving them away as you would giving away thousand-dollar bills. Some of us never get over the rush . . . and never stop looking for excuses to do it again.

Sadly, many people who love pretty things, especially flowering plants, have never even seen a phalaenopsis flower. Only a few of those who _have_ will have seen the flower still attached to a plant. Most people's experience with orchids, if they have any at all, is with the large, showy _cattleyas_ in corsages . . . or _dendrobiums_ or _vandas_ in their mai tais or on a pillow in Hawaii.

So ahead of you, you have the beautiful experience of introducing people to _real orchids_.

A few ground rules to the game first, though.

6.1 BEFORE ANYTHING ELSE

(1) Just before they bloom, take the plants out of the bright light and move them to a cool, shady spot. The flowers will last longer that way. Put them back in their usual growing place when the blooms are gone.

(2) Flame the razor or knife blade you use to cut the blooms. Pass it briefly through a flame to kill any virus, fungi, or bacteria that can infect the plants.

(3) After cutting the blooms or spikes, put them in water at room temperature for at least 3 hours or store them that way until you are ready to use them.

(4) Do not chill the flowers _before_ making them up into corsages or arrangements. The cold makes the stems brittle and they are more likely to break during the making process.

(5) Keep made-up arrangements or corsages chilled before and when not in use. They will last much longer that way.

6.2 SHARING BLOOMS

The simplest way to share the blooms is to cut them and put them in 'water pics'. These are plastic tubes that hold a small amount of water, enough to sustain the flower for a few days. They are available at florists or florists' supply houses. Not very fancy, but the message is the flower, not the container.

A glass tube is the next step up and makes the whole presentation finished and professional. You don't have to apologize for this kind of a remembrance. It is elegant and in good taste. The glass tubes with a spiral base are also available at florist or florists' supply houses.

Bud vases are too big for a single bloom,

but just right for a phal spike or spray. I don't cut many flowering spikes because it usually is too much for an individual presentation. Table arrangements are 'right' for a spike, though.

But, I can't think of a better way to say something nice than a single phal bloom in a glass tube...like hospital visits, for a foyer table, for a great secretary's desk, for your favorite lady barber, and for any of those you'd like to say 'thanks' to in a special way.

6.3 GIFT PLANTS are the next step up in giving away the store. When in bloom, in a decorative basket with its leaves shined, there is no nicer compliment to the receiver. Usually reserved for phal growers or dedicated African violet growers who are being anointed as Ready To Move Up to the big league.

6.4 PHALAENOPSIS ORCHIDS ARE THE BEST OF ALL THE ORCHIDS FOR PERSONAL ADORNMENT e.g. corsages, wristlets (they're coming back), hair adornments, and boutonnieres.

White blooms are available six months of the year including the June-July wedding season when cattleya ('standard' or 'Japhet') orchids generally are not.

Phals are also available in colors more suited to personal adornment than cattleyas. Soft, muted colors are common, but so are the bright spots of color that are needed occasionally...again, in many of the useful sizes. If you see yourself using phal blooms for this purpose, consider that during the plant buying process.

You can choose from plants that will yield blooms ranging in size from half an inch up to five inches in side-to-side measurement. Try that with cattleyas!

Phal blooms also fit well into floral arrangements and a cascading spike of white blooms will add drama and sweep to any arrangement.

Many greenhouse orchid growers sell a few blooms to help offset their utility costs. Florists are usually eager to have a local grower who can be counted on for quick orders when there isn't time to get orchid blooms from the commercial flower market. The quality is usually better, too.

There is something special in having your flowers used on commemorative occasions such as proms, weddings, anniversaries, birthdays, Mother's or Father's Days, and even funerals. You are more involved and ties are made closer...even with only one flower. The flowers become a personal testimony. It is a _nice_ feeling. For special friends, I usually offer, in advance, to provide the orchids for family-member weddings. Their reaction is similar to what you'd expect if you pelted someone with hundred-dollar bills.

6.5 OTHER USES

Try floating cut flowers on water in a shallow, decorative bowl or in a brandy snifter.

Float them in a fountain or swimming pool during special occasions.

Do as the Hawaiians do and put a fresh bloom on the pillow in a guest bedroom.

Make up a 'corsage' and use it as a snazzy decoration on a wrapped gift...in place of a ribbon bow.

Use them in dried flower arrangements. (We have an artist-friend in San Diego who makes the dried flowers into paper from which she makes very special note cards. The flowers are clearly discernible in the paper.)

Use a single flower as part of a place setting for special dinner occasions. . .or a spike as a centerpiece.

Take a flowering plant to the office and share the beauty with friends. The orchids will add a nice, new facet to your image. "I grow orchids" is a conversation-stopper.

An acquaintance, as a student, conducted a small signature-collecting effort to get his name on a ballot. He wasn't very successful, but for years after he would crystalize conversation at cocktail parties by casually remarking "In '58 when I ran for the Senate. . ."

We put flowering plants in the bathroom of the guest room when we have company.

On Mother's Day, I try to remember favorite waitresses with a small, simple corsage.

At flower shows, I try to pick out little, old ladies in the crowd who may never have had an orchid corsage. . .and change that. Try that if you want to feel good about yourself sometime. "Pretty flowers for pretty ladies."

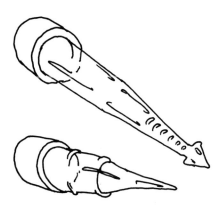

'Water pics' and a tube.

27

SECTION 7.   WHERE DID I GO WRONG?

7.1   WHY WON'T IT BLOOM?

The usual reason why phals won't bloom is a lack of light.

Many new growers take the term 'houseplant' a bit too literally and presume that the phal will need about the same light that a <u>foliage</u> houseplant needs...and then despair the lack of flowers. Fact is, if the phal is given too little light, it will vegetate very nicely and produce pretty, dark-green leaves...and nothing else.

Asking the new grower to guess at what 10% of full sunlight looks like is a bit much, but a reasonably close estimate can save you a whole growing season that may be needed to show that a given spot has not enough light for the plant to flower. One thing I <u>really</u> fret about is that some new growers will give up during that first season and try something else.

So, the guess at what is enough light to make a phal flower is an important guess.

If you have to guess on the wrong side of 10% of full sunlight — which is what the phals need to bloom — guess on the high side.

LET ME QUALIFY THAT COMMENT: A <u>LITTLE</u> ON THE HIGH SIDE.

- A *little* high gets you: Yellow-green leaves and small flowers.

- A *lot* high gets you: A sunburned or even a dead plant.

- A *little* on the low side gets you: Sparse, but large flowers.

- A *lot* on the low side gets you: No flowers, but a pretty, green plant.

The phals will tolerate considerable overdosage of light before getting into any trouble. I'd rather see new growers overdose them a little than underdose them, because at least they see the flowers.

I have never known a new grower to overdose a phal on light except by leaving them in direct sunlight and heat in a parked car with the windows rolled up. When that happens, Zap! The plant is gone.

There are a few other reasons why a phalaenopsis orchid will not bloom given the other recommended cultural conditions, but they are infrequent. Flower spikes may sometimes fold and collapse when splashed with cold water in the winter.

Immaturity or poor health of the plant, of course, will usually deter flowering. Sometimes a plant will flower while it is in bad health as an act of desperation...to keep the species alive. It's a pathetic sight; the poor thing trying to carry on by flowering even when the flowering may rob it of strength it needs to stay alive. It's a jungle out there.

Don't let it happen to your plants. If a sick plant throws a flower spike, cut it off at the base and nurse the plant back to health before allowing it to flower again.

Overly-warm nighttime temps can prevent flowering, too, if they happen during the fall when spikes are normally set. Refer back to the earlier section on temperatures.

7.2 WHY DID IT DIE?

Every phal grower loses a plant now and then. It's not the end of the world if one goes belly-up on you (except when it happens to one of the good ones and then it probably is the end of the world.)

The number one reason why people lose phal plants is dehydration, caused by (1) not enough water and (2) too much water.

I know, that sounds contradictory, but it is true. Too much water leads to root rot...which leads to loss of roots...which cuts off the plant's access to water and voila! a dehydrated plant.

The answer to not enough water is obvious. The answer to too much is not so easy. For openers, water the plant only when the pot feels light...instead of every Thursday come hell or high water. That kind of mentality leads to lawn sprinklers going in a pouring rain...'cause today is the day we water.

Start by hefting the pot and watering it when it begins to feel unusually light. From that experience, set an interval between waterings. Then adjust that interval to allow for cooler, warmer, drier or wetter conditions than normal.

An easier way is to increase the size and number of drainage holes in the pot so you can't overwater. The excess will run out the holes. If you'd like specifics, try giving a 4-inch pot at least one square inch area of drainage holes. Give a 6-inch pot at least two square inches of drainage hole area. Even easier, get some 'azalea' pots for your phals. These have double the normal drainage and are perfect for our needs.

The number two reason why we lose phal plants is bacterial rot.

If water is allowed to stand on the plants after sundown, bacteria may proliferate in the wet spots. That bacteria can harm the plants by causing rot.

The answer: don't allow water to stand on the plants after sundown or during cloudy days.

Water early in the morning on sunny days and not at all on cloudy ones. If you have to water on cloudy days, go ahead and do it, but blow or sponge the water out of the crowns of the plants or turn up the heat or turn on a fan or spray them with a solution of bactericide. (The kind used in swimming pools or spas should do OK if you don't have access to horticultural bactericides. A product called *Physan* does an excellent job...and can be used in many other applications as well. *Listerine,* the mouthwash, will also work in a pinch.) Spray just one leaf and wait a few days to see if an unfamiliar chemical or unknown strength is going to damage the plant.

Harmful bacteria exist on the surface of the leaves and in water. **No water, no bacteria problem.** Got the message? If left unattended, the bacteria will attack the leaf tissue and get inside where they can kill the plant.

If a leaf shows a dark, wet-appearing spot, it may well be bacterial rot. Cut the spot out of the leaf with a flamed, sterile blade...and spritz a little *Listerine* or *Physan* on the open cut.

7.3 WHAT ARE THOSE CRAWLY THINGS?

The number three reason for losing phalaenopsis plants is attack by pests.

Aphids, mealybugs, mites and scale are the

most common pests around phals. After dispatching the nasty little buggers with a spray of *50% Malathion* or *Dursban* insecticide, note which and when pests attacked your plants. Annotate a calendar with the information and 'lead' them by a few weeks in the following year. Be ready for them.

When you spray, do both top and bottom of the leaves. Mites are especially good at hiding under leaves.

If you have only a few plants, a small, soft-bristled brush will do to sweep the insects away.

In a pinch the old standby remedy of soap and water will help rid your plants of insect pests if they start to gang up on you. Mix a teaspoon of dishwashing detergent in a quart of water and spray the whole plant when the pests are on the plant or are expected. Repeat as needed. Rinse and wipe the leaves when the threat is past.

Mealybugs are little cottony masses about a quarter-inch long with hairs sticking out in all directions. Scale are hemispherical brown or white things that, as adults, are stuck permanently in one place. Both are noted for two things: Finding orchid plants and eating them.

ONE PEST YOU MAY NOT SEE, BUT WHICH WILL FIND YOUR PHALS, NO MATTER WHERE YOU HIDE THEM, IS THE MITE.

There are lots of different kinds, but you'll need a magnifying glass to see any of them. You will know when to suspect you have them when leaves start to fall off the plant in frightening numbers in the warm, dry weather. They leave a silvery, stippled surface, usually on the underside of phal leaves. They can destroy a phalaenopsis plant in short order if not checked.

Kelthane, or any compound containing it, is good for mite control. It's an old product, but a good one. There are others, better, but they are not available commonly at most garden suppliers.

Slugs and snails are fond of our phals, too. Mash those suckers, or sprinkle a little snail bait on the surface of the potting medium. Get the granulated form, if you can, preferably containing metaldehyde or *Mesurol.* I find *Cookes Slug-N-Snail* granules effective.

Squirting a half-and-half solution of water and household ammonia on them will also do the job. The only problem with this method is that you must see them to use it...and the little beasties don't always oblige.

Slugs and snails usually won't kill a plant, but will almost always make a mess of it, particularly the flowers...snails relish them.

If you are growing your phals in the house, snails and slugs are not usually a problem, but I've found slime trails on the living room carpet where they've come in from the solarium trying to find an orchid plant. Imagine stepping on one of those at night with your bare feet? Ugh.

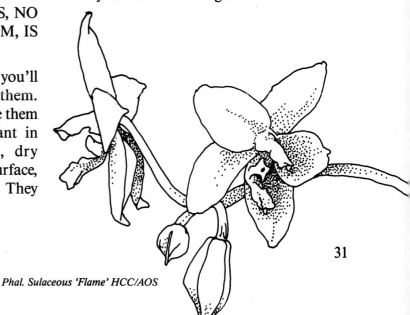

Phal. Sulaceous 'Flame' HCC/AOS

31

SECTION 8.   NOW WHAT?

IF IT DIED, GO BACK TO PAGE 1. If not, congratulations. Press on. This section is for the graduates.

8.1 SOCIETIES

If you haven't already done so, find and join a local orchid society or club, if there is one. (Some garden clubs will have a member or two who grow orchids...if there are no local organized orchid societies.)

These societies can be the source of help, encouragement and ideas. They are basically social groups that will provide you with orchid learning and companionship in a pleasant setting, if that is important to you.

If you don't know where to look for a local orchid society or club, ask a local florist who grows orchids in the area. Or drop a note to the:

> American Orchid Society
> 6000 S. Olive Avenue
> West Palm Beach, FL 33405

There are other orchid groups, but the most structured and organized are affiliated with the AOS. There are many groups outside the US that are affiliated as well.

Membership in a local group can lead you to membership in the American Orchid Society and a window on what is going on in the international arena of orchid affairs. Also, the AOS is the source of many useful books, speakers, and a system for judging orchids for awards in competition with other growers worldwide.

Again, with the local groups, you'll meet a few people with a lot of answers and a lot of people with as few answers as you have. Most societies have education as one of their bylaw-objectives and will do something in that direction.

Some societies have learning groups for new growers. Their meetings usually precede the monthly general meeting.

Most societies have a show-and-tell event at their monthly meetings where growers can show their current bloomers and have them judged in an informal way. It's good practice for later on when you may want to show your plants for AOS awards (Very prestigious)

Many people I've met are hesitant about showing their plants...for all manner of declared reasons. But the down-deep, usual reason is fear of not winning an award and looking foolish in the process.

That's sad, because they deny themselves one of the real joys of any hobby...showing your stuff with that of others. No one wins awards every time, but the more you show, the more times you win. Even if you have only one plant in bloom, show it proudly. We all enjoy beautiful things even if they are not the best in their class. Most of us would be in tough shape if only the best-looking people got any recognition.

Besides, the sight of tables at society meetings crowded with flowering plants is a wonderful sensory overload.

8.2 HYBRIDIZING

Making your own orchid hybrids may not have occurred to you up to this time, but tuck that one in the back of your mind to be brought up when your levels of interest and commitment are right. YOU CAN MAKE ORCHID HYBRIDS...IT'S EASY. It requires a commitment to several years of growing the seedlings before they flower, however. Lab costs for propagation are modest.

If you don't see the kind of phal flower you'd like to see, you can work at changing that...and giving the world something it may not have. Like to have some hybrids, maybe even one with your name, left behind you for future generations to enjoy? Piece of cake.

For further information on this subject and an expansion of the ideas mentioned up to this point in this book and some new ones, I recommend a copy of a more detailed phalaenopsis book... *Culture of the Phalaenopsis Orchid* by Bob Gordon.

It is available from the same source as this book,

> Laid-Back Publications
> 276 East Shamrock
> Rialto, CA 92376

1986 price is $14.95 postpaid.

8.3 STRAIGHT AHEAD

In the cool, quiet hours just before dawn, it has occurred to me more than once that there is a parallel between the emotions experienced in raising children and those experienced in raising phalaenopsis orchids:

• Apprehension — when we are new to caring for a new one of them.

• Pleasure — in watching their development under our care.

• Displeasure — when they don't live up to our expectations...somehow.

• Pride — in their achievements and recognition...a vicarious experience.

• Warmth — in the enjoyment of their progeny.

• Respect — for their age and achievements.

• and Fulfillment — in their passing.

Most of us have the human need for emotional experience. It's all right here. Life in a microcosm of another world.

What role do *we* play? Superparent, perhaps...committed emotionally to improving the breed for the future.

I guess we could do worse.

I'd like to think we would leave the world a better place than when we found it...but our track record hasn't been too good lately.

I want to encourage you, the reader, to use orchid culture as a healthful, relaxing pastime. Contemplating the flowers is a marvelous way to unwind and settle the mind for clearer thinking...to wipe your mental slate clean. Nero Wolfe did. Thirty minutes with your orchids is better for you than two silver bullets after a tough day...any day.

If you have questions, write to me at the Laid-Back address above with a self-addressed stamped envelope and I'll answer them as best I can and as time permits.

Thank you for reading my book.

Welcome to our midst. I hope orchids and orchid friends bring you the same sense of fulfillment and tranquility...that they do for the rest of us.

> —Bob Gordon
> Rialto, California
> September 1986

8.4 SOURCES OF PLANTS AND THINGS:

Boulder Valley Orchids
240-2nd Ave, P. O. Box 45
Niwot, CO 80544

Butterfly Orchids
821 Ballina Ct.
Thousand Oaks, CA 91320

Carmela Orchids*
P. O. Box H
Hakalau, HI 96710

Coqui Nurseries*
P. O. Box M
Bayamon, PR 00620

Feather Acres Nursery
980 Avocado Place
Del Mar, CA 92075

Fennell's Orchid Jungle*
26715 S.W. 156th Ave.
Homestead, FL 33031

Orchids by Hausermann*
2N 134 Addison Rd
Villa Park, IL 60181

J & M Tropicals
Rt 1, Box 619B
Cantonment, FL 32533

Jones & Scully*
18955 S.W. 168th St.
Miami, FL 33187

Kensington Orchids*
3301 Plyers Mill Road
Kensington, MD 20895

Livingston's Orchids*
128 Hughes Road
Watsonville, CA 95076

Miller's Orchids
2021 Margie Lane
Anaheim, CA 92802

New York Botanical Garden
Bronx, NY 10458-5126

Orchid World Int'l*
11295 S.W. 93rd St.
Miami, FL 33176

Petra Orchids (Australia)
P. O. Box 129
Townsville, QLD 4810

Richella Orchids*
2881 Booth Road
Honolulu, HI 96813

Rod McLellan Co.*
1450 El Camino Real
So. San Francisco, CA 94080

Stewart Orchids*
P. O. Box 550
Carpinteria, CA 93013

W.C. Orchids
1389 Friends Way
Fallbrook, CA 92028

Zuma Canyon Orchids*
5949 Bonsall Drive
Malibu, CA 90265

* Have plant lists

SECTION 9.   INDEX